Where Do Goods Come From?

How Is Software Made and Sold?

Bridey Heing

Cavendish Square
New York

Published in 2020 by Cavendish Square Publishing, LLC
243 5th Avenue, Suite 136, New York, NY 10016

First Edition

Library of Congress Cataloging-in-Publication Data

Names: Heing, Bridey, author.
Title: How is software made and sold? / Bridey Heing.
Description: First edition. | New York : Cavendish Square Publishing, LLC, 2020. |
Series: Where do goods come from? | Includes bibliographical references and index. |
Audience: Grades 2 to 5. | Summary: "A book for young readers about how
software is created and then sold to the public"-- Provided by publisher.
Identifiers: LCCN 2019018745 (print) | LCCN 2019021260 (ebook) |
ISBN 9781502650504 (library bound : alk. paper) | ISBN 9781502650481
(pbk. : alk. paper) | ISBN 9781502650498 (6 pack : alk. paper)
Subjects: LCSH: Application software--Development--Juvenile literature. |
Computer software industry--Juvenile literature.
Classification: LCC QA76.76.A65 H44 2020 (print) | LCC QA76.76.A65 (ebook) |
DDC 005.3--dc23
LC record available at https://lccn.loc.gov/2019018745
LC ebook record available at https://lccn.loc.gov/2019021260

Editor: Caitlyn Miller
Copy Editor: Denise Larrabee
Associate Art Director: Alan Sliwinski
Designer: Christina Shults
Production Coordinator: Karol Szymczuk
Photo Research: J8 Media

The photographs in this book are used by permission and through the courtesy of:
Cover Mind and I/Shutterstock.com; p. 5 Wavebreakmedia/Shutterstock.com; p. 6 MicroOne/Shutterstock.com; p. 7 Bloomicon/Shutterstock.com; pp. 8, 16 Uladzik Kryhin/Shutterstock.com; p. 11 Skynesher/E+/Getty Images; p. 12 Omihay/Shutterstock.com; p. 14 Kiatateeti/Shutterstock.com; pp. 19, 23 Rawpixel.com/Shutterstock.com; p. 22 60b/Shutterstock.com; p. 25 Lane Oatey/Blue Jean Images/Getty Images; p. 26 Whitney Hayward/Portland Press Herald/Getty Images; p. 27 Laymanzoom/Shutterstock.com.

Printed in the United States of America

Table of Contents

Chapter 1

All About Software

People use **software** every day. It helps us learn. It helps us work. It helps us talk to each other. Software can do a lot of things. Software lets you type on a computer. It also powers fun games on a tablet. Software plays music on your phone. Taking a picture with your phone uses software too. Software is all around us. It's important to know how it works and where it comes from.

Software, Hardware, and Code

Software tells **hardware** what to do. A smartphone is an example of hardware. A computer is also hardware. The software that tells a piece of hardware how to work is called an operating system. Every computer has one. Tablets and smartphones do too. All this software is made up of **code**. Big programs need lots of code. Microsoft's operating system took about fifty million lines of code to build!

A tablet is an example of hardware.

DID YOU KNOW?

Code is a kind of language. Computers and devices can read it. Every device has a processor. It changes the code into tasks and actions.

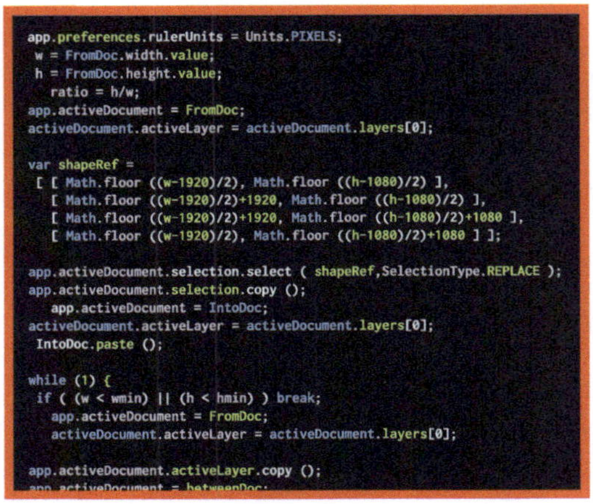

Java is a coding language. This is what Java looks like.

Code is like a sentence that a **device** can read. There are different coding languages. People who make software must choose a language to create code. Python, Java, and C++ are popular languages for software. They are made up of letters, numbers, and symbols. The first version of Minecraft was written in Java. Adobe Photoshop is written in C++. There are many more languages to pick from!

Software Engineers

Software code is made by software engineers. Software engineers write code. They test it too. They make sure devices read code the right way. Many software engineers studied computer programming at school. Some studied software design. Other software engineers teach themselves.

Applications are also called apps. You can see icons for different apps here.

Software engineers work on different projects. They might work on systems. Systems are what makes a device run. They might also work on **applications**. Applications are

DID YOU KNOW?

Ada Lovelace was a mathematician. She created the first computer program in the 1840s. Her work led to the creation of today's software.

Google is an important tech company. Its headquarters is in California.

programs we use on devices. Examples are games or calculators. Sometimes, a whole team of software engineers works on one piece of code. Writing code takes a lot of time! Testing code also takes a lot of people and time.

Our devices work thanks to software engineers. Big companies like Google and Microsoft hire software engineers from all over the world. Their employees work at offices in many countries. Sometimes, companies get very busy. They might need someone with skills no one on their team has. They might want to save money and hire a cheap company. In these cases, they hire smaller companies to create some parts of their software.

Chapter 2

Making Software

Software has changed a lot in the last twenty years. How it is made has changed too. Code had to be written from scratch in the past. Today, it is much easier. Software engineers use programs to create software code. There are also programs that let people who aren't software engineers create code. Even kids can use them.

Designing Code

All software starts with an idea. A software engineer needs to decide what they want software to do.

Sometimes, a company finds a problem and asks for software to fix it. Other times, users ask for something new.

The idea is the first step. The second step is using a special program to create the code. Some programs that create code can only be used by companies. Others can be used by everyone. Members of a team of software engineers will work on different parts

It takes a whole team of software engineers to make software.

of the code. Some might work on the **interface**. The interface is what the user sees on their screen. Others will work on writing the code the computer will read. Sometimes, these team members work in different offices. They might even work in different countries.

Testing

Testing is an important part of creating software. Software has to be tested to make sure it works.

When you play a game, you usually don't find bugs. That's because software gets tested.

Testing needs to happen before software can be sold. A problem with software is called a bug. Software engineer teams use the software and fix bugs.

There are a few steps for testing. Software engineers can do tests while the code is being created. They can also test when it is done. Both ways help catch bugs. Software engineers need to look at the code they wrote to make sure there are no errors in it. Software is tested many times to make sure it works.

There are computer programs to catch bugs. These are called debuggers. There are also people who test the software but don't create it. These people are called QA testers. Sometimes,

DID YOU KNOW?

Most devices cannot run old software. Software needs to be updated on a regular schedule. Updates fix problems. They give users new **features** too.

they are called QA engineers. “QA” stands for “quality assurance.”

Where Is Code Written?

Software engineers write code in a special place. This is known as an integrated development

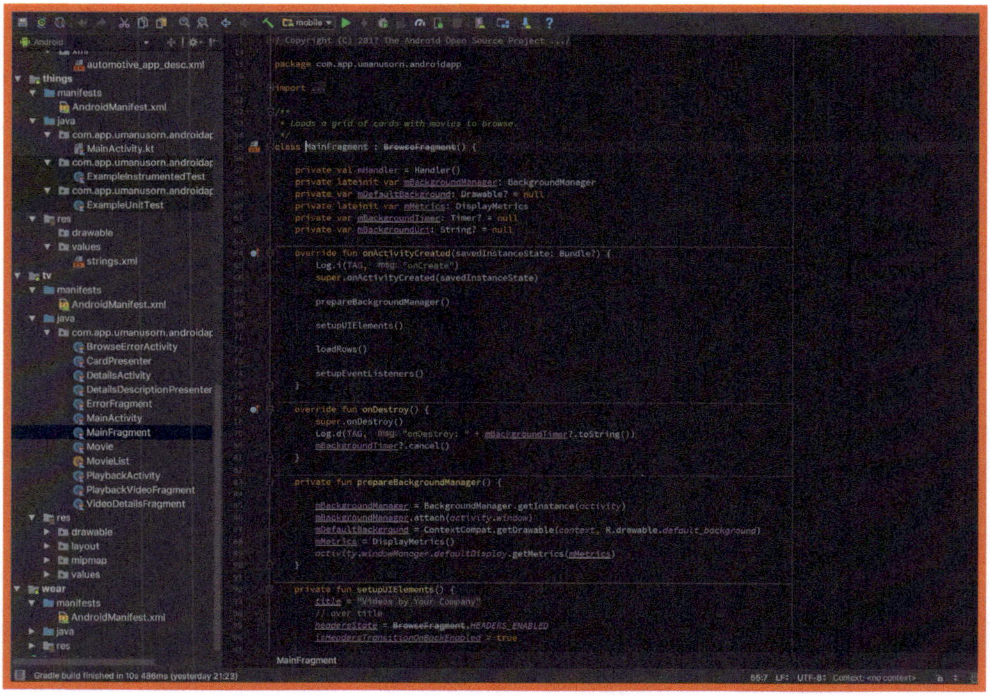

An integrated development environment is used to write code for software. Engineers can write, test, and debug all in one place.

environment (IDE). It looks a little like a notepad program on your computer. It is different because it lets software engineers test their code. It also lets software engineers **debug**. One popular IDE is called Visual Studio.

Working Together

Creating software is a worldwide business. Cities in the United States are home to companies that create software. Other countries also play a big role in creating software. Germany, India, the Netherlands, the United Kingdom, and China have large software companies.

Software made in one country might be different from software in another country. This is because different countries need different kinds of software. Software engineers in a country that doesn't have

Silicon Valley in California is home to a lot of software and technology companies, like Google and Apple.

many banks might create software so people can use their phones to send money.

Companies in different countries work together to create software. This means people in different countries can learn from one another. They also gain new skills.

DID YOU KNOW?

Silicon Valley in California is home to many important software companies. Google and Apple are based in Silicon Valley. Software engineers from around the world work there.

Chapter 3

Selling Software

Software is made around the world. It is also bought and used around the world. Software from the United States is used in hardware in countries like Japan and Egypt. This means software is a large industry.

Today, devices that use software are becoming cheaper. More people can buy them. Software is being bought and used by more people every day. Billions of dollars are spent on software and the devices that use software every year.

Most people download software over the internet.

Software Is Important

Software is used in many products. Some of them are bought by people and families, like cell phones. A lot of software is used by companies, governments, or other

DID YOU KNOW?

Microsoft is one of the largest software companies in the world. It was founded by Bill Gates and Paul Allen in 1975. It is worth more than $850 billion.

groups. Sometimes software companies need to buy software!

Software can be used to do a lot of things. Software helps pilots fly airplanes. It helps schools keep track of attendance. Software engineers are always coming up with new ways software can help us.

Licensing

All software is licensed. This means that software makers decide how their software can be used. Some can only be sold by one company. An example is the software in Apple products. This is called **proprietary** licensing. Other companies, like Google, provide **open-source** software. That means anyone can use their software. Some programs, like Microsoft Office, can only be bought from the company that makes it.

How We Buy Software

Most software is sold online. It is sold through downloads or updates to devices. People used to buy software on disks. Now, people download software right to their devices over the internet.

Not all software is bought outright. Some software is available through a subscription. This means a user can pay to use a program. They can use it for a week, a month, or years. After someone's subscription is over, they can't use the software anymore.

DID YOU KNOW?

Many software companies that sell subscriptions try to sell customers longer subscriptions by offering big discounts.

How We Use Software

We buy and use a lot of software. A lot of software is sold to larger companies. Software is also in products everyday people buy in stores. Some products have special software that makes them popular, like smartwatches.

Computers and cell phones advertise their software. Companies talk about how fast their phones and computers are. They also talk about

Apple makes popular software that powers computers, iPhones, smartwatches, and more.

programs that are included. Companies like Apple and Google are able to sell their products based on their software.

Computer software gets updated regularly.

Some software is not marketed at all. A lot of devices get regular updates. Computers, cell phones, and tablets all update their software. That means that people do not have to buy anything new. The device will alert the user when an update is ready. Some updates even happen without users knowing about them.

Chapter 4

Global Connections

Software is an important part of our world. People around the world are thinking of new ways to use software. They are also thinking about new ways to make it easier to use.

Helping People

People in a lot of places can get cell phones. They can't always get computers. Many software engineers are working to make software that runs on cell phones. Software engineers are also working on programs to make coding easier. The next step is no-code programming. This is software that doesn't use code. No-code programming makes it easier for people to learn how to make software. Software engineers are also finding ways to make software work on different devices, such as smartwatches.

Video chat software connects people across long distances.

DID YOU KNOW?

The Internet of Things (IoT) is a new use for software. It means putting special hardware into everyday items, like refrigerators. Then, they can be controlled by software.

This app gives users recipes to make with their leftovers. This reduces food waste!

Software can also be used to solve problems. Software engineers are using software and technology in new ways. They use it to reduce food waste. Software can also help journalists share information. It can help us talk to loved ones around the world.

Software companies try to protect users' privacy. They work to keep hackers from stealing information about users.

Privacy

There are some worries about software. One is privacy. People are thinking about how to protect it. Software can sometimes be hacked, or broken into. Hackers take the information stored in software.

Some companies also use software to get information, or data, from users. Information can be sold. Sometimes a user doesn't know their information has been sold. Countries are passing laws to protect users' privacy. In many European countries, people have the right to be forgotten. This caps how much data can be kept about them.

The Future of Software

The future of software will be even more global than it is today. Companies around the world are working together. They are finding new ways to test software. They are also finding new ways to get it to users. They are even finding new ways to keep users safe. Software has an exciting future!

DID YOU KNOW?

Artificial intelligence (AI) is a form of software that is meant to allow machines to think like people. It is still being **developed**. Scientists and engineers have done a lot of work in AI.

Glossary

applications Programs that run on a device.

code The instructions that make up software.

debug To get rid of bugs in software.

developed Made and tested.

device An object that uses software.

features New or special parts of a product.

hardware Devices like computers and cell phones.

interface The way a program or a device's screen looks to users. It is what users type or click on.

open-source Able to be used by anyone.

proprietary Only able to be used by one company.

software Programs that tell a device how to work.

Find Out More

Book

Robinson, Peg. *How Computers Work*. Everyday STEM. New York, NY: Cavendish Square Publishing, 2019.

Websites

Computer Software | HowStuffWorks

https://computer.howstuffworks.com/computer-software-channel.htm

This website explains how software works.

Hardware and Software

https://www.khanacademy.org/computing/computer-science/how-computers-work2/v/khan-academy-and-codeorg-hardware-and-software

This is a video about hardware and software.

Index

Page numbers in **boldface** refer to images. Entries in **boldface** are glossary terms.

About the Author

Bridey Heing is an author who writes about books, history, and current events. Her other books include *How Are Cars Made and Sold?* Heing lives in Washington, DC. She likes to read, hike, and go to museums.